Merry Christmas Dad.
Lots of Love.
from Da
l (JK).

I shall be the One to walk with you
For you need someone by your side.
I shall be the One to talk
For you need to listen
And to listen while you talk.
I shall carry your load when it is heavy
And carry you when you can walk no more.
I shall lift the cup to your lips
when you thirst
And feed you when you are hungry.

At first you will not recognize me
For I shall be as familiar to you
As you are to yourself
For you shall know me as the cloak you
wear
And the sandals on your feet.

When the day dawns that you know
me by name....
Then shall our journey begin.

LYNN NEW ©

Protected

You're quite safe with me
I'll never let you go.
You asked me into your life
On you my light I'll throw.
Your mind at times in turmoil
The pressures seem too great
Don't feel you've been deserted,
Just stand, be calm and wait.

You're quite safe with me
I will not let you down.
Once I wore an earthly robe,
A ring of thorns my crown.
So when at times you're tired,
Your foot steps weary tread
Don't feel you can't move forward
For you are safely led.

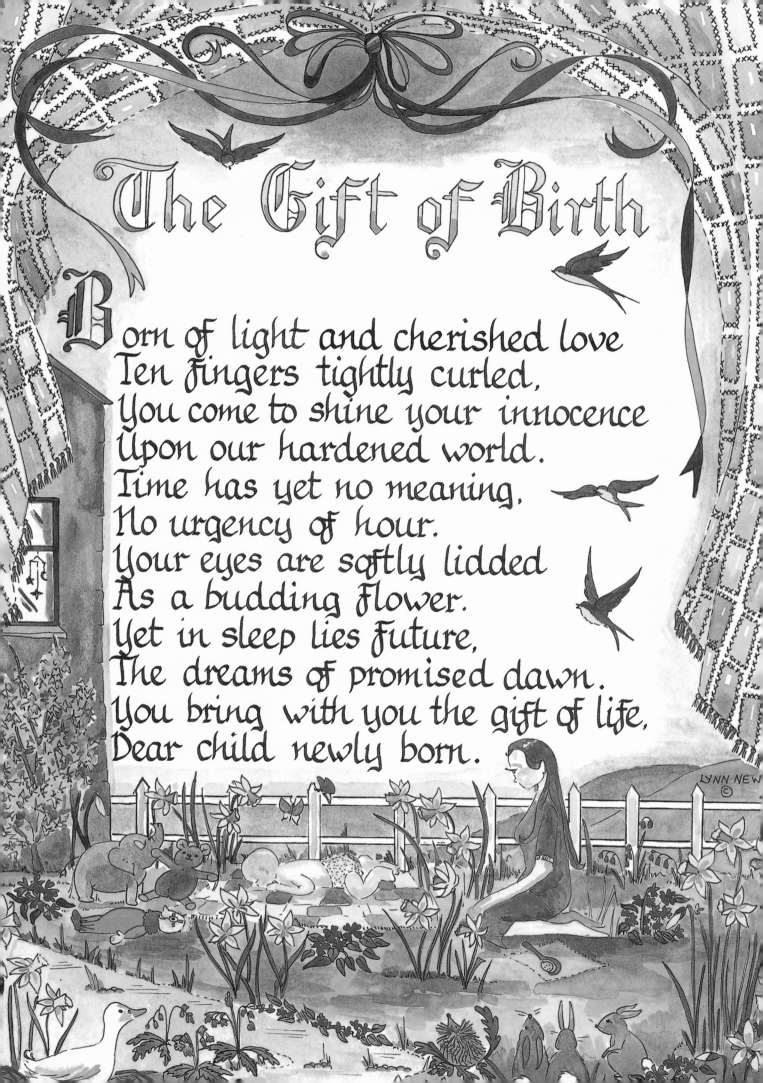

The Gift of Birth

Born of light and cherished love
Ten fingers tightly curled,
You come to shine your innocence
Upon our hardened world.
Time has yet no meaning,
No urgency of hour.
Your eyes are softly lidded
As a budding flower.
Yet in sleep lies future,
The dreams of promised dawn.
You bring with you the gift of life,
Dear child newly born.

Step Renewed

I travelled on my pathway
Knowing not the journey's end.
I walked with dull monotony
And turned at every bend.
I questioned not the reason,
Each foot fell as the last
And soon my longed for future
Became my distant past,
For everything I'd dreamt of
Like every challenge met
Had been, in part successful,
I was content, and yet
Something deep inside me
Questioned why I strode
This pathway I'd not chosen
This dry and dusty road.

Until one day in thoughtfulness
I halted on the track;
What point in going forward?
Yet I could not turn back.
I was weary and emotional.
I cried, as if in prayer.
The answer first I doubted,
I felt the Lord was there.
"The meaning for your journey
Through life is yet unshown.
Take consolation in the fact
You never walk alone."

LYNN NEW ©

My Prayer

Dear Father in Heaven
Please hear my prayer,
I need to know now
You'll always be there.
I give you my eyes
To widen my sight
    For I'm scared of the shadows
    That fall with the night.
Please make me less anxious
Help me understand
I sometimes need courage
To give you my hand;
    Faith that You'll hold me
    To wipe tears I've cried.
    Knowledge You love me
    And stand by my side.
Please share with me patience
Through my night and my day
And give me the words
That help me to pray;
    To feel Thee draw closer
    To cast away fear
Knowing Your Presence
Remains ever near.

LYNN NEW ©

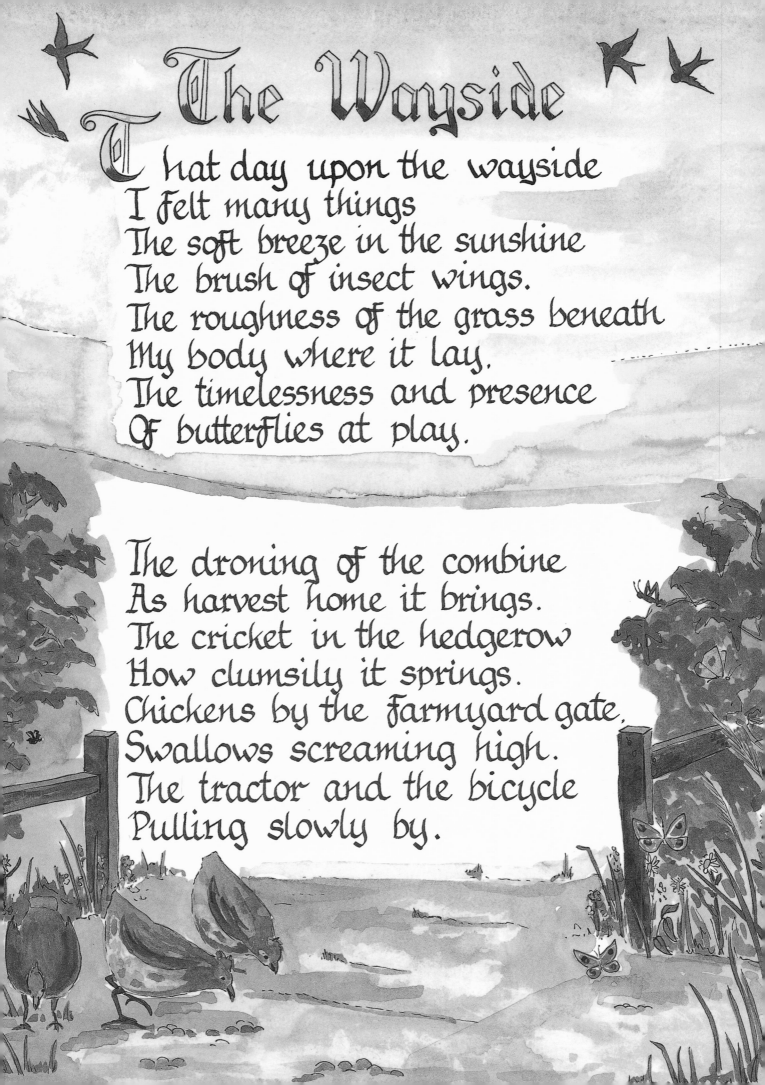

The Wayside

That day upon the wayside
I felt many things
The soft breeze in the sunshine
The brush of insect wings.
The roughness of the grass beneath
My body where it lay.
The timelessness and presence
Of butterflies at play.

The droning of the combine
As harvest home it brings.
The cricket in the hedgerow
How clumsily it springs.
Chickens by the farmyard gate,
Swallows screaming high.
The tractor and the bicycle
Pulling slowly by.

Basking beetles in the heat
While I rest in shade.
By the statue of Our Lord
I found I quietly prayed.
Nature's choir sung to me
"All creatures great and small".
For every insect, bird and flower
It's true, God loves them all.

That day upon the wayside
I learnt many things
Most of them about myself
As if my soul had wings
For I had touched serenity
While resting in the sun.
That day beside the dusty road
My soul and I were one.

LYNN NEW ©

Each Step

When grey clouds swirl around your head
And mists obscure the view,
When every forward step you take
Returns in circle new
When every time your hope is raised
Then dashed on rocks below
And people say each challenge met
Is one from which to grow.
Time then to stand and patient be
Yet do not feel afraid
The straightest and the truest path
Is one that's surely laid.
Each stone is turned and firmly placed
By hands that aren't your own.
Be guided, soon the way ahead
Will lovingly be shown.

LYNN NEW ©

Blessed Wings

Late autumn sun may tint your wings
Though winter chills the heart.
Too soon the song of summer's passed.
Too soon you must depart.
Yet one last day of glory holds
Your gift of velvet light
Upon your painted wings at rest.
Pray God you'll not take flight.
For summer's child of soundless wings
Your day draws to its close.
Hold for me a while yet
Your painted, promised pose.
Then when you drop away from life,
For angels claim their own,
Let me, in turn give thanks and praise
The butterfly now flown.

LYNN NEW ©

The Lantern Carrier.

One night I walked to the end of my road
Where a man stood, unknown to me.
He held up a light to show me the way
Held it high and bid I should see.
Although I drew near I could not make out
His face, though familiar did seem.
I stood by his side, attracted, absorbed
Like a moth in the light of a beam.

"Neighbour," he said, in a voice calm and sure,
"I've watched for you nightly in vain.
You walk down the pavement, head bowed
and intent.
I've watched you through moonshine
and rain.
At last you are drawn and caught in my
light.
Will you stand and take comfort from me?
'Tis the Light of the Lord that shines from
this lamp
And all who look up truly see."

Yet I did not know this neighbour of mine.
"Are you new, I've not seen you before?"
"How could you miss me, how could you
                              not know?
Friend I live only next door.
For I am the neighbour who spills out the
                              light
From the lantern to lighten your load.
Also the Lord who patiently waits
At the corner of your darkened road."

The Table Setting

When there's no answer to your question
No ear to hear your voice.
No voice to give an answer
No decision, only choice.
No Friend when you are needy
Only folk who say they care.
Stand still, look round, be certain
Our Lord is always there.
You do not need to see Him,
Or even call His name
Just recognise His presence
In your heart and put to shame
The doubt that has been kindled
By each circumstance you face
Lay a setting at your table,
Let Him take His rightful place.

LYNN NEW ©

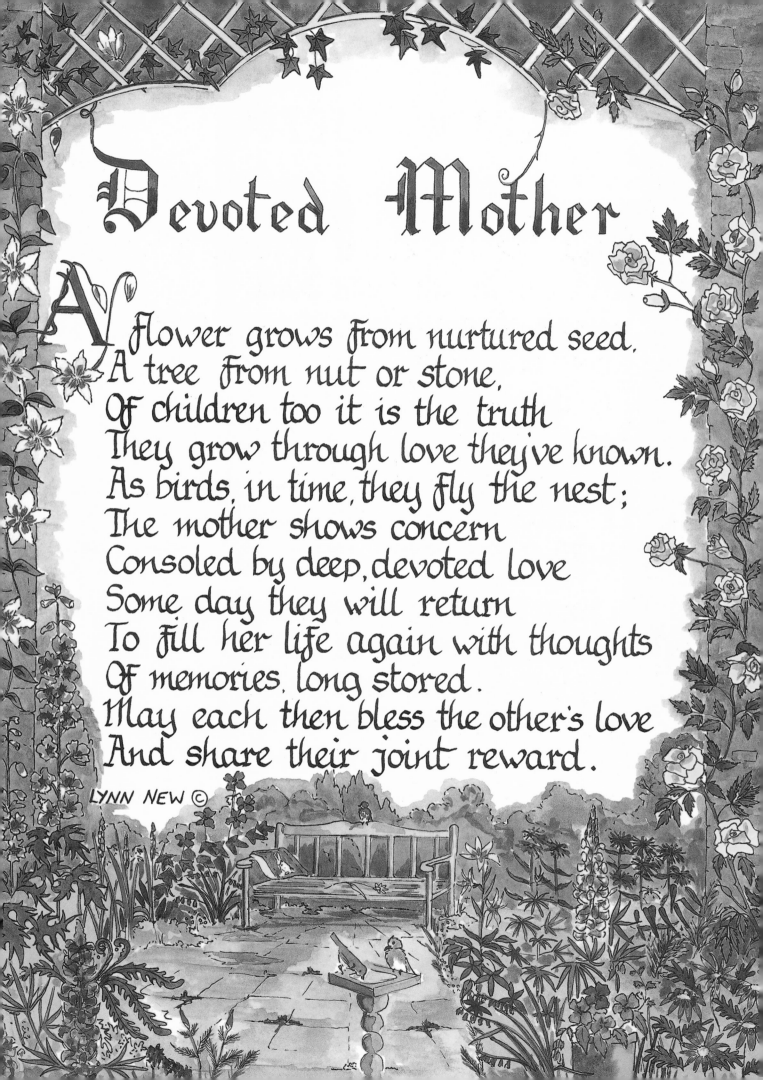

Devoted Mother

A flower grows from nurtured seed,
A tree from nut or stone,
Of children too it is the truth
They grow through love they've known.
As birds, in time, they fly the nest;
The mother shows concern
Consoled by deep, devoted love
Some day they will return
To fill her life again with thoughts
Of memories, long stored.
May each then bless the other's love
And share their joint reward.

LYNN NEW ©

Remembered

Still the blood red poppies grow
And yet it's all been said
Words of strength and valour true
Upon our boys, long dead.
All the tears have surely dried
Their memory washed clean.
The family photos, faded now
Of lads no longer seen

They sleep in foreign sunshine
They rest in rural rain.
Tended by the honourable
And honoured, most by name.
Left in peace a life time
That generation plucked
By the bullet and the bomb,
By the mud that sucked.

And yet as seeds from crimson blood
The field poppies grow
By the hedgerows where they fell
Not by the grave marked row.
Tended now and manicured
These regiments of stone
Names and dates from history
Though some are marked "unknown".

Most days are solitary spent
For life, like years, pass on.
There are many who forget
The soldiers who have gone.
Though some still make the pilgrimage
And stand with heads bowed low
Remembering the lads they lost
Where field poppies grow.

LYNN NEW ©

RIFLEMAN
F. FARMER
48741
21·NOV·1918

Your Guiding Hand

Teach me to stand in the shade
of others
But carry my own light.
To walk the unknown pathway
Till dawn dissolves the night.
To hold on to my vision; that
daylight dream
When things go wrong, or so
would seem.
Teach me to love, God's word, not mine
To make from sacking coarse a
garment fine.
To find in shallow words a worthy
thought
And every lesson learnt, one to be
taught.
And when I have a question, yet
can not understand
When the answer is before me...
...Hold out Your guiding Hand.

LYNN © NEW

The Father

The love between the Father
And his child takes the form
Of a strength forever gentle
That weathers every storm.
That each may grow in wisdom
And so shall surely learn
Respect can not be ordered
It's something all must earn.
As the child who is cherished
Becomes an adult overnight
The wise and caring Father
Guides his youngster to the light.
While the child, in turn, shows patience
And accepts the Father's hand
In the knowledge both are equal
And each other understand.

LYNN NEW ©

Little Lamb

Come children, swiftly gather
A story must be told
Of a lamb in winter
Who strayed far from the fold.
The others did not notice,
They looked on her as nought,
But the shepherd counted out
                His lambs
And for her surely sought.

The winter wind was blowing
And snow lay on the hills.
The little lamb was weakening;
The harshest season kills.
Our shepherd battled onward
He would not lose His sheep.
He found her quietly huddled,
As if she were asleep.

"Come little lamb, awaken now,
My Father's calling you.
He will give you sustenance
And a shelter new."
Know that caring shepherd
Is the Son of God in guise
And we, like sheep protected
Are children in His eyes."

LYNN NEW ©

Searching

We look for the Light of the Lord
Yet we stand in the warmth of His sun.
We pray that new life will begin.
Have Faith, it's already begun.
We search for the jewel in the crown,
Yet His head was pressed by the thorn.
Still we ask for an unfaded cloak
But are given the one He has worn.
All that we have is enough,
We are gifted with all that we need.
Why ask for the harvest of corn
While already possessing the seed.

LYNN NEW ©

Let Thy Light Shine.

The church was still and silent
No organ played.
The congregation left
But still he stayed.
While all around him
Shadows stated claim
He stood alone and wanting
This man without a name.
What frown on furrowed brow?
What weight to bear?
He came to find his God
While no one else was there.

He had not learnt to pray,
He could not understand.
He only knew he needed God
To hold his empty hand.
While in this quiet reflection
He prayed he would be shown
That God was standing by him,
That he was not alone.
The sun was slowly slipping,
Slanting shadow fell.
Just how long he stood there
It was hard to tell.
He was feeling disillusioned
Forgotten in his woe
Empty hearted and neglected
He made as if to go.

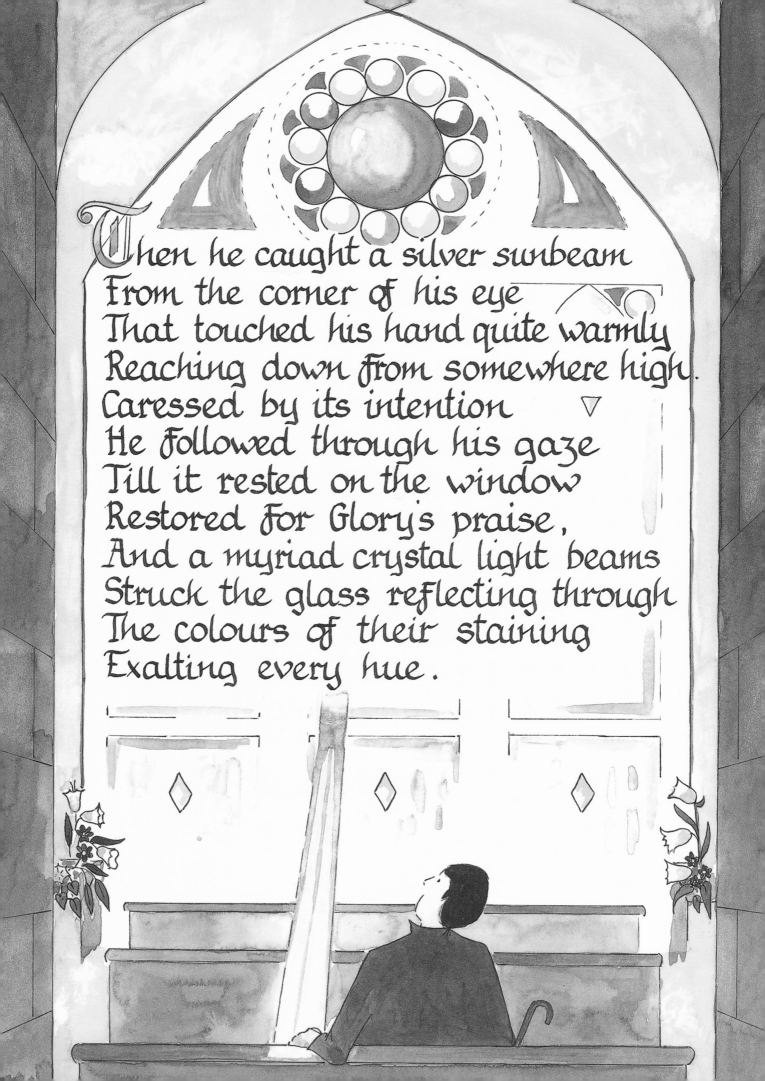

Then he caught a silver sunbeam
From the corner of his eye
That touched his hand quite warmly
Reaching down from somewhere high.
Caressed by its intention
He followed through his gaze
Till it rested on the window
Restored for Glory's praise,
And a myriad crystal light beams
Struck the glass reflecting through
The colours of their staining
Exalting every hue.

Now the leaded captured beauty
Caught his heart as well as eye
As if his God had spoken
"Behold, for I am nigh".
For love had lit the window
That for life had been restored
And the man was blessed with
healing
By the Presence of Our Lord!

Tailor-made.

You can not learn from others.
Each have their point of view.
The lessons which are set in life
Are tailored just for you.
Perhaps you have a question,
You have been given choice.
No right or wrong to guide you
Just a deep and inner voice.
You'll make your own decision
Without reward or blame.
For each it will be different,
No circumstance the same.
Yet when you find the answer
The problem then is solved
And the reason for its lesson
Will have been resolved.

LYNN NEW ©

The River's Story

Sit upon my river bank
Allow your mind to float
Away from all the cares you hold~
Hush... listen to each note
Of trickled water over stone
Of breeze between each reed
All your cares to wash away
Down stream where currents lead.
Can you not hear this river's song?
Listen while I sing
My music holds a lesson,
Serenity to bring.
I do not need to worry
Which way I shall wend
From source until the sea I flow
With energy to spend.
I bear no thought or reason
For circumstance will state
The speed of flow, the forcefulness,
The outcome of my fate.

Go with the current of your life,
Flow and think of me.
Though bounded by my bordered
banks
I am Forever Free.

LYNN NEW ©

The Poppy

The poppy in the Field short grows
Through petals red the light it throws
And though no taller than the rest
This poppy's tired, it's stood the test.
The Farmer passes through that Field
And looks upon the poppies yield.
He picks one, chosen from the land
And holds it firmly in his hand.
No different from the ones that grow
He lifts it high that He may show
The glory of this precious flower
Acknowledging its final hour.
As the field of poppies sway
To send their sister on her way
The Farmer's hand is raised to bless
The poppy with the Lord's caress.

LYNN NEW ©

Pages
Through Ages

Life is an open book, you must
Turn and read each page.
Hurry not or skip a line,
Each chapter is an age.
The first few are of childhood
The last, in truth, must be
The passing of the spirit
Through Eternity.
Treasure every moment,
Digest every line
For book and life, as one they read,
A life time to define.

A chapter of contentment
Perhaps one of dis-ease
On some your eyes will struggle,
Others only please.
This book is held by all souls,
Placed in every hand,
Its up to us to read it through
And to understand.
Each volume will be different
No two can be the same
But the one that's placed before you
In gold, now bears your name.

The Sanctuary

Sit with me, oh Lord
For just a little while.
I find it hard to pray,
It's not my style;
But closer draw
And my companion be
For that way Lord
I can talk to Thee.

With eyes fast shut
Hands clasped in prayer
It's difficult to visualize
You are standing there.
But within my garden
Eyes wide though lowered must
I can feel Your presence
And in that I trust.

LYNN NEW ©

Column of Life

I stood at the bottom of the
                    "Column of Life".
It was high, it was stone, it was straight.
I looked all around to find me a door
For the vision, now formed, had come late.
I noticed a door, carved, rusted and strong
And someone had lent me the key.
It turned in the lock and opened ajar
Gave me entrance and bid I should see.

I climbed with a dream of reaching the top
Though it was dark and the steps were
                    uneven.
So many souls had climbed them before
No doubt with the same dream and reason.

I could not look down the spiralling depth
For the past was soon left behind.
I had to look up to the arrows of light
Which shafted on steps so inclined.

As I grew weary my dream became tired
I rested my hand on the wall.
There wasn't a rail to help pull me up
But I knew even then I'd not fall.
Once in a while it was almost too much
Then a landing of stone I would reach
And I could take pause and rest there
                              awhile
And from it I'd learn and I'd teach.

As I stood still for a minute or two
I could hear climbing footsteps behind
And a voice softly calling "I'm coming -
                              please wait.
Help me climb this stairway; be kind."
So this I did, then climbed on my way
After encouraging those in my wake.
Soon, once again my legs became tired
I thought no more I could take.

I called to the one before me, above.
Called for wisdom, for strength and for
                              light.
The footsteps above stopped where they fell
And waited till onward I'd fight.

The Column of Life is a vision to climb
Till one day the top we will reach,
But while on that journey that spirals
around
Remember, we learn and we teach.
The Footsteps we hear on the stairs far above
Give us help and encourage us through.
Those climbing behind need a hand on
their way
That someone, by chance, could be you.

LYNN NEW ©

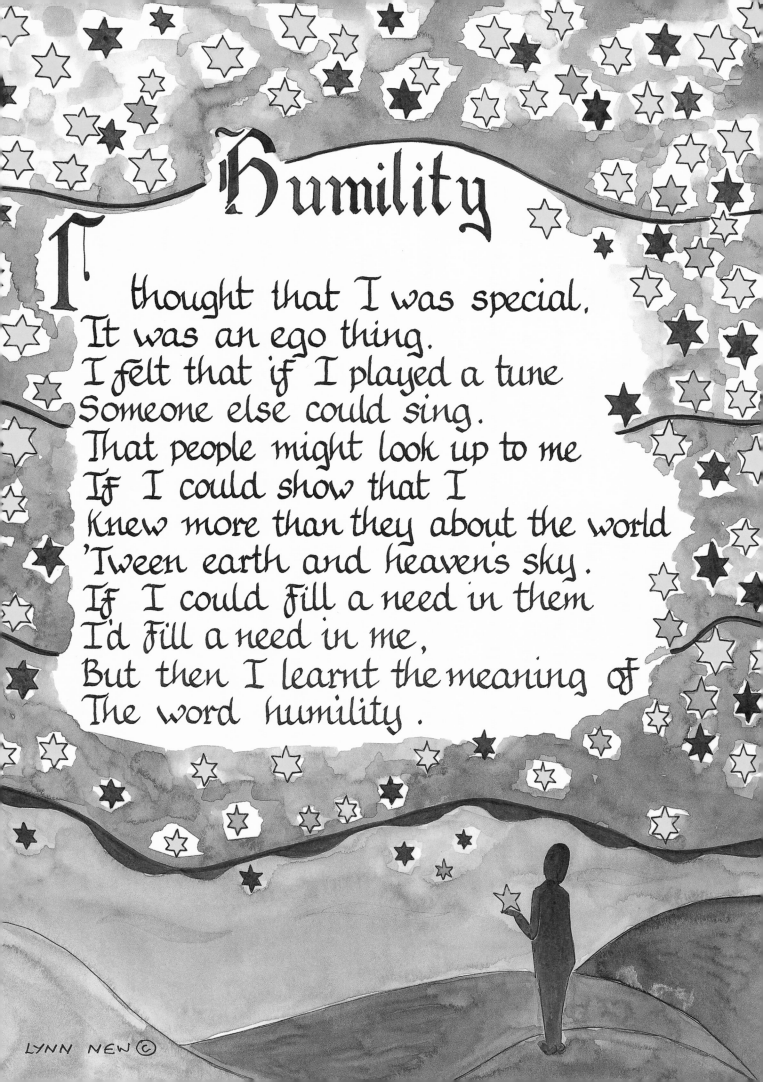

Humility

I thought that I was special,
It was an ego thing.
I felt that if I played a tune
Someone else could sing.
That people might look up to me
If I could show that I
Knew more than they about the world
'Tween earth and heaven's sky.
If I could Fill a need in them
I'd Fill a need in me,
But then I learnt the meaning of
The word humility.

LYNN NEW ©

Maternity

I have no children
But I have a heart.
I stand with others
And yet I stand apart.
No mother now
In whom I can confide.
No loving partner
Lying by my side.
I have no roots~
The past has all been dealt.
The future is unknown,
As yet unfelt.
I sometimes feel afraid,
I can not lie
The earth is large
And larger still the open sky.

No reason now to stay
Yet none to go.
My friends can't understand,
They can not know.
Deep within this woman
A mother cries
For her unborn child.
Can no one realise?
Maternity is not a word
It is a soul expressed.
Though some may never be fulfilled
Others may be blessed
And those like me who recognize
This maternal law
Shall carry love in cradled arms
For others, evermore.

LYNN NEW ©

Life's Tide

Flotsam and jetsam
Low tide then high,
Caught in the current
Beached there to dry.
Tumbling stones
Ridges of sand
A lifetime exposed
By destiny's hand.
How many stories
Uncovered, untold?
How many secrets
The tide to unfold?
Each tiny pebble
Each worn stone
Mirrors the image
Of life, we have known,
For we're governed by fate
And the turn of the tide
Sculptured by life
And the currents we ride.

The Balance

Does heaven lie beyond the skies
Or safely in your heart?
True hell lies in this world we live
And both must play their part.
The scales of life fall equally
A balanced compromise
For what is light without the dark
Or day without night skies?
Know your hell but heaven too,
Experience them both,
But try each time the darkness falls
To visualize your growth.

Hope

A Falling Feather in the Frost
Perhaps another bird is lost
Or moulting early in the spring
Discarded now from strengthened wing.
All hush from sentinels of oak
Adorned by misty, silken cloak.
Old winter wears its silver shroud
While fog horn mourns it, long and loud.
This world subdued and lost, the view.
The palest sun can not break through.
Late winter covers all I see...
Yet spring will come eventually.

LYNN NEW ©

Meadow Moments

I lie on my back in the meadow
With eyes fast-fixed on the sky
And I watch in the peace of His presence
Those fluffy white clouds passing by.
Then my mind starts to formulate
                              questions
The answers to which I don't know.
As I lie in this tranquil setting
Where beneath me buttercups grow.

Why aren't I always this peaceful?
Why must I fight to survive?
Today as I lie in this meadow
I'm only too glad I'm alive.
Here the warmth of the sun takes the
                              shadows
Dissolving them into the light.
As the clouds are dispersed on their
                              journey
Now vanquished and put to flight ...

Now God must have heard my mind's
question
Though I had not voiced it aloud
But His answer was written above me
In every dissolving white cloud.
'Tis the sun that fades down the shadows
'Tis His Light that answers our prayers
So take heart when you need the
answers
Know that the One above cares.

Coming Home.

Friends, don't be down hearted
My family, please don't mourn.
Do not now be sad for me,
My coat was tired and worn.
I've left it with the memory
Of every one of you.
Now it's time to rest in peace,
Enjoy God's chosen view.
I've lived with many faces
Fate wove its twisted way
Now at last I am myself
And that I now can stay.
Remember me quite kindly
With love, not tears you've cried.
I walk in Light with God above,
Yet still stand by your side.

LYNN NEW ©

Grace for God

For what we're about to receive
For what we're about to consume
Please make us be thankful oh Lord,
Please make us also have room;
Our want is greater than need
And our lives are fuller than most,
While others are crying for bread
We look down our noses at toast.
All merchandise sold in the shops
Can be ours if we sign on the line
But what more could I possibly want
Than my hand holding Yours....
　　　　　　　　holding mine.

LAUGHTER
KINDNESS
PATIENCE
FAITH
WILL
COMPASSION
LOVE
WISDOM
GNESS
TRAINATTON
HUMOUR
TRUST
HOPE
YOU
DETER
COURAGE
STRENGTH
PEACE
SELF-WORTH
TRUTH
HUMILITY
RESOLVE
CARING
WONDER
HONESTY

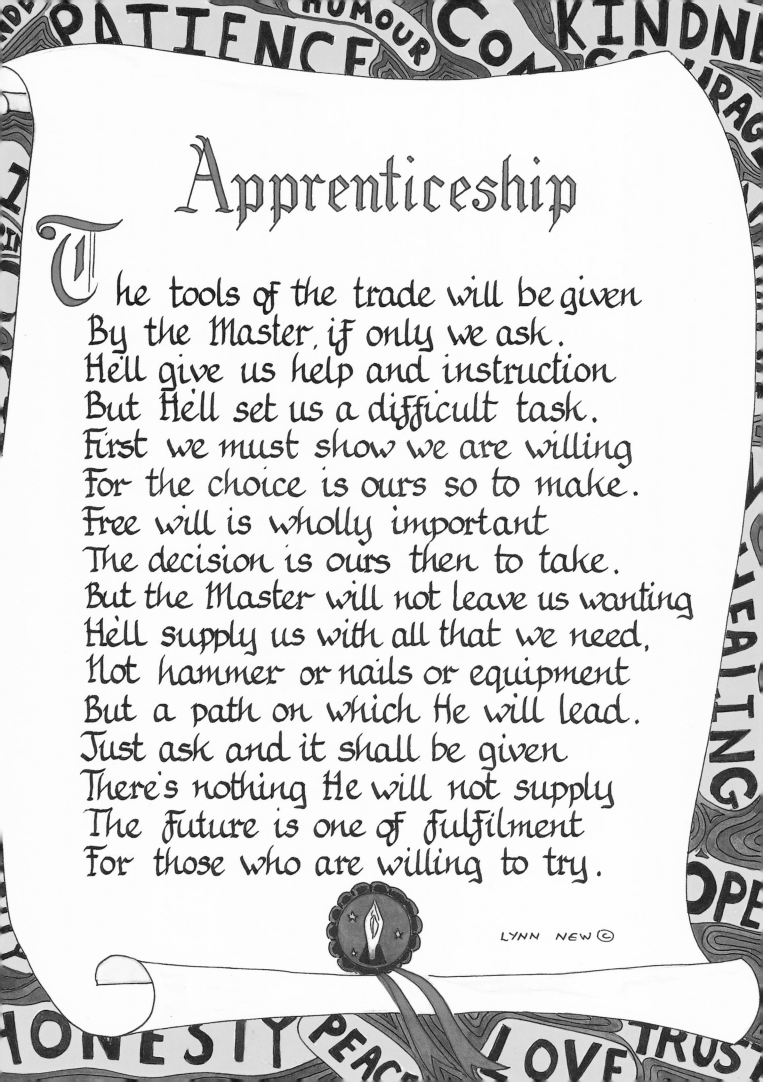

Apprenticeship

The tools of the trade will be given
By the Master, if only we ask.
He'll give us help and instruction
But He'll set us a difficult task.
First we must show we are willing
For the choice is ours so to make.
Free will is wholly important
The decision is ours then to take.
But the Master will not leave us wanting
He'll supply us with all that we need,
Not hammer or nails or equipment
But a path on which He will lead.
Just ask and it shall be given
There's nothing He will not supply
The Future is one of Fulfilment
For those who are willing to try.

LYNN NEW ©

Laughter Lines

We must talk to God
And our laughter share
It's not blasphemy,
It brings a healing air.
We're told He is all things to man.
It's that which sees us through;
But we must show our happiness
And that way say "Thank You."

THANK YOU

HAPPINESS

JOY

LYNN NEW ©

My Inspiration.

The inspiration behind the verses is the first and most vital step towards the creation of my book, without which its journey could not have been made. I would like to share with you the thoughts which triggered the verses and the inspiration which gave birth to the poetry.

1. I SHALL BE THE ONE. *Inspired in the stillness of dawn when my need for confirmation and guidance was great.*

2. PROTECTED. *Written originally to encourage a friend though I think I had a little higher help in this, don't you?*

3. THE GIFT OF BIRTH. *The birth of Lorna. A new life born against all odds.*

4. STEP RENEWED. *Inspired by my own thoughtfulness and search.*

5. MY PRAYER. *For my absent friend in hospital at the millennium.*

6. THE WAYSIDE. *Pausing in a warm country lane in the Loire valley.*

7. EACH STEP. *Written with concern for a friend and neighbour.*

8. BLESSED WINGS. *The old wall in my garden catches the last summer sun and the late butterfly.*

9. THE LANTERN CARRIER. *Inspired by my friend who was to be baptised the following day. Written at night while the city slept: a time of great peace.*

10. THE TABLE SETTING. *I needed a caring word. Look at the illustration. Can you interpret the poem.*

11. DEVOTED MOTHER. *She is of course the inspiration.*

12. REMEMBERED. *Written while visiting the 2nd. World war cemetery in France while tracing a family member. The past and present merged.*

13. YOUR GUIDING HAND. *Inspiration comes from your heart when there is no one to visibly give it.*

14. THE FATHER. *For the father of teenage children and his commitment.*

15. LITTLE LAMB. *The greatest pieces need little explanation. Jesus is the loving shepherd.*

16. SEARCHING. *Do we need as much as we think we do to survive?*

17. LET THY LIGHT SHINE. *Commissioned by a lady to be read at the dedication service of a stained glass window for her Welsh chapel. It became the story of a man's search for God. The window reflected God's light, touching the man and restoring his faith with love.*

18. TAILOR-MADE. *A little philosophy of life.*

19. THE RIVER'S STORY. *Written in text ten years ago. When compiling the book I thought it was worthy of a poem.*

20. THE POPPY. *This was written for my aunt's funeral. I had nothing appropriate and wrote this on the London train going to the funeral.*

21. PAGES THROUGH AGES. *This one seemed like common sense to me.*

22. THE SANCTUARY. *I can be close to God and nature in my garden.*

23. COLUMN OF LIFE. *This piece was inspired by day to day life, even with four pages I had to leave a lot out!*

24. HUMILITY. *Its simplicity says it all. A profound statement.*

25. MATERNITY. *Inspired by my heart. It explains that love must have expression and that the childless will fulfil that expression of love through other ways in life.*

26. LIFE'S TIDE. *The sea is at the end of my road... I have to be inspired.*

27. THE BALANCE. *A statement of life, enjoy the illustration.*

28. HOPE. *A winters morning, a falling feather for inspiration.*

29. MEADOW MOMENTS. *Time to watch the clouds; I had to be on holiday.*

30. COMING HOME. *I returned my mother home to her final rest. This poem was written for the service.*

31. GRACE FOR GOD. *A little "pop" at commercialism.*

32. APPRENTICESHIP. *A little help for those who try hard.*

33. LAUGHTER LINES. *Humour is a great healer and a perfect way to end my book.*